Sexy French

French

Getting it on in France

Emma Burgess

SUMMERSDALE

Summersdale Publishers Ltd
46 West Street
Chichester
West Sussex
PO19 1RP
UK

www.summersdale.com

Printed and bound in the EU.
By Nørhaven Paperback A/S, Denmark
ISBN: 184024 240 X

Contents

No matter what country you're in, the way to a woman's heart is through her bra. And the way to a man's is through that little slit in his pants.
Emma Burgess

Introduction
including some clichéd generalisations and insults

France contains a population of more than fifty million, not all of whom are habitual dangerous drivers and hairy-armpitted horse eaters. But it's possible that - whilst visiting the country of hard wine, soft cheese and headless aristos - you might encounter someone with whom a romantic liaison seems like a good idea. Should such a situation arise, chances are you'll be so drunk and incoherent that even your native language will become a struggle.

This book will help you focus your thoughts towards the inevitable phrases needed in order to seduce a stinky foreigner. It will also prove invaluable in getting rid of them the next day and explaining to the doctor that it now hurts when you wee.

Sometimes, though, things aren't so clear cut. Events can spiral out of control and - *sacrebleu* - you might end up getting hitched to some Gallic geek quite by mistake. Despair not! This nifty tome covers all eventualities and will even aid you in your journey home...if you sober up in time to see sense.

So on your next *sortie* across the Channel, use your stiff upper lip as a shelf on which to keep this book (plus a photo of Charles de Gaulle perhaps?) and you'll have guaranteed success with our sweaty, stunted neighbours.

P.S. Before a French reader feels compelled to jump on his metaphorical high-horse and accuse me of xenophobia, go and metaphorically grill it instead. *Bien cuit*.

Getting started

Before you stick your silver tongue down the Gauloise-stained throat of a French person, you need a *soupçon* of grounding in the boring basics of the language. After all, there's quite a difference between *oui* and *non*, and you'd better get used to hearing the latter if you're going to give the chat-up lines in the next chapter a go.

Some useful numbers

(but not all of them because that would take up half the bloody book)

One Un	**Five** Cinq	**Nine** Neuf
Two Deux	**Six** Six	**Ten** Dix
Three Trois	**Seven** Sept	**Sixty-nine** Soixante-neuf
Four Quatre	**Eight** Huit	

Months of the year

January Janvier	**May** Mai	**September** Septembre
February Février	**June** Juin	**October** Octobre
March Mars	**July** Juillet	**November** Novembre
April Avril	**August** Août	**December** Décembre

Days of the week

Monday	**Thursday**	**Sunday**
Lundi	Jeudi	Dimanche
Tuesday	**Friday**	**A week**
Mardi	Vendredi	Une semaine
Wednesday	**Saturday**	**A year**
Mercredi	Samedi	Une année
	The weekend	
	Le weekend	

Other useful words

France
La France

The French
Le français
La française
Les franchouillards

A frog
Une grenouille

Boyfriend
Petit ami

Girlfriend
Petite amie

Romance
L'amour (m)

Lover
Un(e) amant(e)

Lovesick
Amoureux qui
   languit d'amour

Loveydovey
Trop tendre

Lovesong
Un chanson
   d'amour

9

Sexy French

No
Non

Sex appeal
Le sex-appeal

The Channel
La manche

Please
S'il vous plaît

Sex fiend
Un obsédé

Yes
Oui

Sex
Le sexe

Thank you
Merci

Getting it on...
a cornucopia of corny chat-up lines

Unless you skip straight to the 'Getting Desperate' chapter of this book and restrict the use of your language skills to France's internationally acclaimed red light districts, you're going to have to chat someone up before getting to the(ir) interesting bits.

Breaking the ice with a stranger is hard enough in your own language, and approaching a Frog that you've never met before with the aim of bedding them presents a particular challenge.

The chat-up line you use must be tailored to the precise situation in which you find yourself, so the following phrases are grouped according to some common scenarios.

Generic:

I could make you very happy.
Je pourrais vous rendre très heureux.

Do you believe in love at first sight?
Croyez-vous au coup de foudre?

Fancy a champagne breakfast?
Aimez-vous un petit déjeuner au champagne?

Excuse me, I'm new around here. Please can you direct me to your bedroom?
Excusez-moi, je suis étranger/ère. Où est votre chambre, s'il vous plaît?

Come and see my etchings.
Venez voir mes esquisses.

CHAT-UP LINES: PURE CHEESE

To him:

Is that a baguette in your pocket or are you just pleased to see me?
Est-ce que c'est une baguette dans votre poche ou êtes-vous heureux juste de me voir?

I'm not wearing knickers.
Je ne porte pas de culottes.

Would you like to feel my hooters? They're real.
Voulez-vous toucher mes nichons? Elles sont vraies.

I've had a boob-job.
J'ai eu la chirurgie d'augmentation mammaire.

I'm quite small, but you look as if you'd fit perfectly.
Je suis tout à fait petit, mais vous regardez comme il que vous vous adapteriez parfaitement.

CHAT-UP LINES: PURE CHEESE

To her:

If I said you had a beautiful body would you hold it against me?
Si je disais que vous-aviez un beau corps le presserez-vous contre moi?

What's a girl like you doing in a place like this?
Que'est-ce qu'une fille comme vous fait dans un endroit comme ceci?

I'm a postman, so you can always rely on me to deliver a large package.
Je suis facteur, ainsi vous pouvez toujours compter sur moi pour fournir un grand module.

I would like to father your children.
Je voudrais engendrer vos enfants.

Do you want to play my organ? It's got some great rhythms.
Voulez-vous jouer mon organe? Il a quelques grands rythmes.

CHAT-UP LINES: PURE CHEESE

15

Sexy French

Generic:

Can I buy you an ice-cream?
Puis-je vous acheter une glâce?

Can I borrow your bucket and spade?
Est-ce que je peux emprunter votre seau et pelle?

This is a nudist beach, you know.
C'est une plage naturiste, vous savez.

Put some of that sun-cream on my back.
Massez-moi avec cet écran soleil sur mon dos.

Save me! I'm drowning in a sea of love.
Sauvez-moi! Je me noie dans la mer de l'amour.

CHAT-UP LINES: ON THE BEACH

To him:

I didn't believe in Greek mythology until now, but I guess you must be Poseidon. Your trident is certainly big enough.
Je n'ai pas cru en mythologie grecque jusqu'ici, mais je devine que vous êtes Poseidon. Votre trident est certainement assez grand.

Is that a pedalo in your trunks or are you just pleased to see me?
Est-ce un pedalo dans vos maillots de bain ou êtes-vous heureux juste de me voir?

Nice pecs.
Beaux pectoraux.

Your swimming-trunks are see-through.
Vos maillots de bain sont transparents.

You might recognise me from Baywatch. Do you get that over here?
Vous pourriez m'identifier à Baywatch. Voyez-vous cela d'ici?

17

CHAT-UP LINES: ON THE BEACH

Sexy French

To her:

I'm a photographer for a famous model agency. Can I take your photo? Maybe without the bikini top?
Je suis photographe pour une agence de modèles célèbres. Est-ce que je peux prendre votre photo? Peut-être sans le haut?

Nice legs. When do they open?
Vous avez des belles jambes. Quand s'ouvrent-elles?

I should rub cream into those.
Il faut que je frotte la crème sur tes seins.

I'd put up with sand in my crack for you.
J'endurerais sable entre mes fesses pour vous.

My nob's had too much sun today. Would you mind if it took shelter in you?
Ma bite a eu trop de soleil aujourd'hui. Est-ce que cela vous dérangerait s'il prenait l'abri dans votre trou?

Generic:

Would you like to dance with me?
Voulez-vous danser avec moi?

They say a good dancer moves well beneath the sheets as well.
On dit qu'un bon danseur est un bon baiseur aussi.

I'd like to dance a slow one with you.
Je voudrais danser lentement avec vous.

What sort of music do you like?
Quelle sorte de musique aimez-vous?

I'll ask if they have any Charles Aznavour.
Je demanderai s'ils ont quelquechose par Charles Aznavour.

CHAT-UP LINES: DOWN THE DISCO

To him:

I will only dance with you if you remove the onions from around your neck.
Je danserai seulement avec vous si vous enlevez les oignons autour de votre cou.

Can I dance around your béret?
Est-ce que je peux danser autour de votre béret?

I'll be your private dancer.
Je serai votre danseur privé.

Take me to the nearest fire station and I'll pole dance for you.
Trouvez-moi la station de sapeurs pompiers près d'ici et je danserai érotiquement pour vous.

Would you mind supporting these while I dance?
Est-ce que cela vous dérangerait de supporter ces seins pendant que je danse?

CHAT-UP LINES: DOWN THE DISCO

To her:

This dance requires me to stick my nob in you. May I have the pleasure?

Cette danse exige d'insérer ma bite en vous. Est-ce que je peux avoir le plaisir?

Every time you do that move, I can see your knockers.

Chaque fois que vous faites ce mouvement, je peux voir vos nichons.

This ultraviolet light is great isn't it? I can see right through your top.

Cette lumière UV est formidable n'est-ce pas? Je peux tout voir à travers votre chemisier.

Isn't it painful when you bounce?

N'est-ce pas douloureux quand vous rebondissez?

In the event that this strobe lighting induces epilepsy, I will be here to find your tongue.

Au cas où cet éclairage de signal d'échantillonnage induise l'épilepsie, je serai ici pour trouver votre langue.

CHAT-UP LINES: DOWN THE DISCO

Sexy French

Generic:

Let me buy you a drink.
Puis-je vous offrir un verre?

Do you believe in sex before lunch?
Croyez-vous au sexe avant le déjeuner?

Love on the rocks?
Amour sur les rochers?

Let's save this ice for later when we're really hot.
Gardons ces glaçons pour plus tard pour quand
nous serons vraiment chauds.

Where is the toilet, please?
Où sont les toilettes, s'il vous plaît?

To him:

Would you like to buy me a drink?
Aimeriez-vous m'offrir une verre?

Have you got anything with which to stir my drink?
Avez-vous quelque chose pour remuer ma boisson?

The more I drink, the more good looking you get.
Plus je bois, plus vous devenez beau.

Is that a glâcée cherry in your pocket or are you just pleased to see me?
Est-ce que c'est une cerise glacée dans votre poche ou êtes-vous juste heureux de me voir?

Stop drinking: I'm not impressed by brewer's droop.
Cessez de boire: je n'aime pas l'abattement de brasseur.

CHAT-UP LINES: AT THE BAR

23

To her:

I want to drink champagne from your navel.
Je veux boire du champagne de votre nombril.

Are you sure you're over sixteen?
Êtes-vous sûr que vous-avez seize ans?

Can I get you a slow, comfortable screw or would you like a cocktail first?
Est-ce que je peux vous obtenir une baise lente et confortable ou aimeriez-vous un cocktail d'abord?

Let's go somewhere that serves proper lager...like England.
Allons quelque part où la bière est bonne...comme l'Angleterre.

Let's get some more drinks in and I might start to fancy you.
Obtenons encore plus de boissons et je pourrais commencer à vous aimer.

Generic:

Have you brought the massage oil?
Avez-vous l'huile de massage?

How do I find the adult channels on the TV?
Où se trouve les canaux d'adulte sur la TV?

Shall we flick through the ubiquitous Gideon's Bible together (and other euphemisms)?
Nous lisons la bible du Gideon omniprésent ensemble (et d'autres euphémismes)?

Are you going all the way in this lift?
Est-ce que vous allez jusqu'au bout dans cet ascenseur?

Shhh! The walls are quite thin.
Tais-toi! Les murs sont comme du papier.

CHAT-UP LINES: AT THE HOTEL

To him:

Let me massage your ego, among other things.
Laissez-moi masser votre ego et les autres choses.

Would you like to tie me to this four-poster?
Aimeriez-vous m'attacher à ce lit à baldaquin?

I'll run us a bath. Oh, look! There's a jacuzzi here too.
Je nous coulerai un bain. Ah, regard! Il y a un jacuzzi aussi.

Take these bags up to my room and I'll be in bed in a mo.
Prennez ces sacs jusqu'à ma chambre et je serai au lit dans un moment.

Are you here for business or pleasure? I'm here for your pleasure.
Êtes-vous ici pour des affaires ou le plaisir? Je suis ici pour votre plaisir.

CHAT-UP LINES: AT THE HOTEL

To her:

I've booked a double room in the name of Mr and Mrs Smith.
J'ai réservé une chambre pour deux personnes au nom de M. et de Mme Smith.

How would you like your eggs in the morning?
Comment aimez-vous vos oeufs le matin?

I've ordered champagne and oysters from Room Service.
J'ai commandé le champagne et les huîtres du service d'étage.

I fancy a three-in-a-bed romp. Shall I ask the maid if she wants to join us?
J'envie d'un ménage à trois. Dois-je demander à la femme de chambre de nous joindre?

Let's see how much we can stain these sheets.
Voyons si nous pouvons souillons ces draps de lit.

Generic:

Excuse me, I'm lost. Will you help find me?
Excusez-moi, je me suis perdu. Pouvez-vous
m'aider à me trouver?

**I know one shouldn't speak to strangers in the
street, but you are so strange I couldn't resist.**
Je sais qu'on ne devrait pas parler aux étrangers dans la
rue, mais vous êtes si étrange je ne pouvais pas résister.

**Excuse me, I'm doing a survey to find my ideal
partner. Would you like to go to bed with me?**
Excusez-moi, je fais une étude pour trouver mon
amant(e) idéal(e). Voulez-vous coucher avec moi?

**Is there a public toilet here where we can get to
know each other better?**
Y a-t-il des toilettes près d'ici où nous pouvons
nous connaître mieux?

Have you ever done it in public before?
Avez-vous déja eu des rapports sexuels en public?

Getting it on...a cornucopia of corny chat-up lines

To him:

Can you help me with this street map? I'm a woman, so I can't read it.
Pouvez-vous m'aider avec ce plan de ville? Je suis une femme, donc je ne peux pas le comprendre.

Mind the gap...between my legs.
Attention au trou... entre mes jambes.

Could you please help me with these heavy shopping bags?
Pouvez-vous m'aider à porter les sacs de provisions s'il vous plaît?

My stiletto is stuck in the pavement: please can you help me?
Mon stiletto était coincé dans le trottoir: pouvez-vous m'aider, s'il vous plaît?

I am raising money for charity by selling kisses.
Je gagne de l'argent pour la charité en vendant des bisoux.

Sexy French

To her:

What a coincidence: this is a one-way street and so is my arse.
Quelle coïncidence: c'est une rue à sens unique et mon cul aussi.

Could you please help me with these not very heavy shopping bags?
Pouvez-vous m'aider avec ces sacs à provisions qui sont d'ailleurs pas trop lourds?

That's a nice dress. Would you mind standing over this air vent?
C'est une robe intéressante. Est-ce que cela vous dérangerait de vous tenir au-dessus de cette mise à l'air libre?

Let me help you over the road.
Je vous aiderai de l'autre côté.

Can I borrow your phone? I need to tell my friends in England that French totty rules.
Est-ce que je peux emprunter votre téléphone? J'ai besoin de dire à mes amis en Angleterre que les filles françaises règnent.

Getting it on...a cornucopia of corny chat-up lines

Generic:

Is this seat taken?
Est-ce que ce siège est pris?

Shall we share a taxi?
Partagons-nous un taxi?

Have you ever made love on a train?
Avez-vous jamais fait l'amour dans un train?

Follow that cab! I've just spotted my future partner.
Suivez ce taxi! J'ai juste vu mon futur amour.

Can I give you a lift?
Est-ce que je peux vous conduire?

CHAT-UP LINES: ON THE MOVE

To him:

Can you help park my car? I have no spatial awareness.
Pouvez-vous m'aider à garer ma voiture? Je n'ai aucune conscience spatiale.

I was the inspiration for the Eurotunnel, you know.
J'étais l'inspiration pour l'Eurotunnel, vous savez.

I didn't realise Adonis had to travel on public transport with us mortals.
Je ne réalise pas qu'Adonis voyage sur le transport en commun avec nous mortels.

Is there room for me on the back of your moped?
Est-ce que je peux voyager sur votre moto?

You have a bike! What a coincidence: that used to be my nickname.
Vous avez un vélo! Quelle coïncidence: c'était mon sobriquet.

To her:

Can I give up my seat for you, or would you like to sit on my lap?
Est-ce que je peux renoncer à mon siège pour vous, ou aimeriez-vous vous asseoir sur mes genoux?

Have you ever done it in a 2CV?
L'avez-vous jamais fait dans une Deux Cheveux?

You don't look old enough to drive.
Vous ne semblez pas assez vieux pour conduire.

Would you like to help me steam up my car windows?
Aimez-vous m'aider faire la vapeur dans ma voiture?

Put your hand on the gear stick. A bit more firmly perhaps. Mmm, that's good.
Mettez votre main sur le bâton de vitesse. Un peu plus dur peut-être. Mmm, c'est bon.

Generic:

Can I share your couchette?
Est-ce que je peux partager votre couchette?

**Even though you've obviously not washed for a
fortnight, I still fancy you.**
Vous ne vous êtes pas lavé pendant une quinzaine
de jours, mais je vous aime encore.

Our trains back home smell nearly as bad as yours.
En Angleterre nos trains sentent presqu' aussi
mauvais que les votres.

You look even better than your passport photo.
Vous êtes plus joli que votre photo de passeport.

Let's go skinny-dipping.
Nagons aux naturels.

To him:

That's an impressive erection you have there.
C'est une érection impressionante que vous avez là.

Golly, what a big tent you have!
Zut alors, quelle grande tente vous avez là!

I have a terrible sense of balance: help steady me while I wee.
J'ai un sens terrible de l'équilibre: assistez-moi à faire pipi.

Would you like to roast my marshmallow?
Voulez-vous rôtir ma guimauve?

Please don't do that - there are children here.
S'il vous plaît ne le faites pas - il y a des enfants ici.

To her:

Would you like to chomp on my sausage?
Voulez-vous boucher ma saucisse?

You appear to be having trouble with your flaps. Would you like me lend you a tent peg?
Est-ce que vous avez une problème avec vos lèvres labiales? Voulez-vous emprunter mes chevilles de tente?

Can I introduce you to my verucca?
Est-ce que je peux vous présenter ma verrue?

You can use my hole in the ground if you like. It's not yet full.
Vous pouvez utiliser mon trou dans la terre si vous aimez. Il n'est pas encore plein.

Your tent or mine?
Votre tente ou la mienne?

Generic

I was planning on having sex tonight. Would you like to join me?
Je voudrais avoir du sexe ce soir. Voulez-vous me joindre?

I can fulfil your sexual fantasy.
Je peux accomplir votre fantasme sexuel.

Fuck me! You're sexy.
Merde alors! Vous êtes très sexy.

I am no longer infected.
Je ne suis plus infecté.

I guess a shag's out of the question?
Une baise: c'est possible?

CHAT-UP LINES: THE UNSUBTLE APPROACH

To him:

Gosh, your feet are big. Is the rest of your body in proportion?
Merde alors, vos pieds sont grands. Le reste de votre corps est-il dans la même proportion?

I have a pierced tongue.
J'ai une langue percée.

The sight of you is making me slightly moist in the pant region.
La vue de vous me rend légèrement moite dans la région de ma culotte.

I swallow.
J'avale.

I'm a really easy lay.
Je suis façile.

To her:

Excuse me, would you mind terribly if I gave you one up the arse?
Excusez-moi, puis-je vous enculer?

You won't need to fake orgasms with me.
Vous n'aurez pas besoin de truquer des orgasmes avec moi.

Can I flick your bean?
Est-ce que je peux effleurer votre haricot?

My fingernails are clean.
Mes ongles sont propres.

Nice jugs!
Beaux seins!

CHAT-UP LINES: THE UNSUBTLE APPROACH

Getting stuffed...
on the food of love

French chefs are renowned the world over
for their superior arrogance. That's why when
you go to France you'll find very little trace of
international cuisine. Their chips look like
Toulouse-Lautrec's nob and certainly won't
come wrapped in last night's edition of Le
Figaro. Even their supermarkets still don't sell
proper bread, milk or cheese.

If you're looking for a restaurant to take your
date to, you might be lucky and find
something akin to a traditional English curry
house, but otherwise you're going to have to
make do with French food.

Beware of the basic differences over there
when ordering from the menu. For instance, if
you order steak, and would prefer the meat

not to be still twitching from the
executioner's stun gun, ask for it to be *bien
cuit*. Even then, don't expect the chef to have
done much more than stick it on the radiator
for a couple of minutes.

Key words:

A gourmet
Une fine-gueule

A greedy guts
Un cochon

To eat
Manger
Bouffer

To be hungry
Avoir faim
Avoir la fringale

Food, grub
La nourriture
La bouffe

French food:

Bread
(that will go stale before you've left the shop)
Du pain (m)
Une baguette

Chips
Des frites (f)

Garlic
L'ail (m)

Frog's legs
Des cuisses de grenouilles (f)

Cheese
(that will stink out the boot of your car)
Du boursin

Horse burger
Un hamburger (don't be fooled)

Onion soup
La soupe d'oignon

Sexy French

Mussels in wine sauce
Des moules marinières

Pizza
Le visage d'un jeune homme français
Une pizza

Snails
L'éscargots

Slugs
(I have no conclusive evidence that *les franchouillards* eat them, but I bet they've given it some thought)
Les limaces (f)

Sparrow on a spit
(bit like chicken-in-a-basket but without much chicken or basket)
Poulet rôti
Édith Piaf

Uncooked cow
Le rosbif
Le bifteak

Ice cream
Une glâce

Hair pie
Une tarte au poil

Water
De l'eau (f)

Coffee
Un café

Tea
Une tasse de thé (m)

Hot chocolate
Un chocolat chaud

Coke
Un coca

Wine
Du décapant

Phrases:

I'm so hungry I could eat a horse.
Je suis si affamé que je pourrais manger un cheval.

That love-making has left me weak. Let's get a snack.
Le fait de faire l'amour m'a aplati. Faisons un casse-croûte.

You are a glutton for love.
Vous êtes un goinfre pour l'amour.

Would you like a pizza and a shag?
Voulez-vous une pizza et une baise?

Can you help me with this menu?
Pouvez-vous m'aider avec ce menu?

I am famished. Let's get a slap up meal.
J'ai faim. Obtenons un gueuleton.

I'm not eating these snails: I will never want oral sex again.
Je ne mange pas ces escargots: je ne voudrais jamais avoir du sexe oral.

Don't try and tell me frogs' legs are an aphrodisiac.
Ne me dites pas que ces cuisses de grenouilles sont
un aphrodisiaque.

**We'll have those leftovers later. In the meantime, I
want to feast on you.**
Nous mangerons ces rogatons plus tard. En
attendant, je te mangerai.

**Anyone would think you've just finished a sex-
marathon. You're really shovelling it in.**
N'importe qui penserait qu'on a juste terminé un
sexe-marathon. Vous mangez comme un cochon.

**Waiter! Can we have the bill please. We've got
some love to make.**
Serveur! L'addition, s'il vous plaît. Nous allons faire
l'amour.

**These melons look like your knockers. Only your
knockers are much firmer.**
Ces melons ressemblent à vos nichons. Mais vos
nichons sont plus solides.

Can I cover you in crème fraiche and lick it off?
Puis je vous couvrir de crème et la lécher?

47

Getting your kit off

French types are less shy about their bodies than we are. Exposed tits are not thought to be offensive, for instance, and can be seen in full glory even in prime time television adverts. So you'd think it would be an easy thing to persuade a French bird to pop them out, wouldn't you? Unfortunately, things are never quite that simple. You may still have to woo, charm and flatter her before she'll let you get your sweaty palms inside her *soutien-gorge*.

Thankfully, undressing a French man is a much easier task. Take him to dinner and, as soon as he's wiped the last trace of horse's mane from his mouth, he'll be naked and pouncing on you. Remember to apologise to the waiter before leaving.

Her clothes:

Bikini
Un bikini

Blouse
Un chemisier

Bra
Un soutien-gorge
Un balconnet

Knickers
Des culottes (f)

Dress
Une robe

Nightdress
Une chemise de nuit

Panties
Un slip de femme

Sexy French

Stockings
Des bas

Skirt
Une jupe

Suit
Un ensemble

Suspenders
Les jarretelles (f)

Swimsuit
Un maillot de bain

His clothes:

Pants
Un slip

Shirt
Une chemise

Tie
Une cravate

Waistcoat
Un gilet

Unisex garb:

Coat
Un manteau

Hat
Un chapeau

Jacket
Une veste

Jeans
Un jean

Jumper
Un pullover

Pyjamas
Un pyjama

Sandals
Les sandales

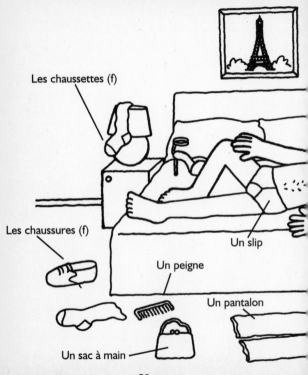

Les chaussettes (f)

Les chaussures (f)

Un slip

Un peigne

Un pantalon

Un sac à main

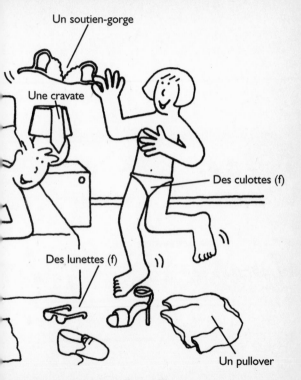

Un soutien-gorge

Une cravate

Des culottes (f)

Des lunettes (f)

Un pullover

53

Shoes
Les chaussures (f)

Shorts
Un short

Socks
Les chaussettes (f)

T-shirt
Un tee-shirt

Trousers
Un pantalon

Accessories:

Belt
Une ceinture

Bracelet
Un bracelet

Comb
Un peigne

Chastity belt
Une ceinture

Cufflinks
Des boutons de manchettes (m)

Earrings
Des boucles d'oreilles (f)

Glasses
Des lunettes (f)

Hairbrush
Une brosse à cheveux

Hairpiece
Une postiche

Handbag
Un sac à main

Sexy French

Handcuffs
Des menottes (f)

Handkerchief
Un mouchoir

Lipstick
Rouge à lèvres (m)

Make-up bag
Une trousse de maquillage

Medallion
Un medaillion

Necklace
Un collier

Pearl necklace
Du sperme au cou
(probably best not to ask for that in a shop)

Ring
Un anneau

Sling
Une écharpe

Sunglasses
Des lunettes de soleil (f)

Watch
Une montre

Wallet
Un portefeuille

Generic phrases:

Let's get naked.
Déshabillons-nous.

Where can we buy a gimp mask?
Où pouvons-nous acheter un masque de boiteux?

Let's play strip poker.
Jouons au poker de bande.

I'm going to slip into something more comfortable.
Je vais porter quelque chose plus confortable.

I don't wear underwear.
Je ne porte pas de sous-vêtements.

To him:

I seem to have my hair caught in your zip.
J'ai coincé mes cheveux dans votre fermeture
éclair.

Call me old fashioned, but I prefer a man not to
wear socks and sandals...in bed.
Appelez-moi une vieille schnoque mais je préfère
un homme qui ne porte pas des chaussettes et des
sandales...au lit.

I don't think I'll wear underwear with this dress. It
might be too restrictive.
Je ne me pense pas que je porterai des sous-
vêtements avec cette robe. Elle pourrait être trop
restrictive.

I'd love a pearl necklace.
J'aimerais un collier de perle.

Those jeans accentuate your bulge.
Ces jeans accentuent votre cambrure.

To her:

I wish I were your bra.
Je voudrais être votre soutien-gorge.

You might as well take all your clothes off: I've got x-ray vision.
Déshabillez-vous complêtement: j'ai une vision de rayon X.

Getting into your knickers is like storming the Bastille...only slightly more bloody.
Entrer dans vos culottes sont aussi difficile que de penetrer la Bastille... mais un peu plus sanglant.

You're telling me they're knickers? Tooth-floss more like. Come floss my teeth!
Vous me dites que ce sont des culottes? La Dent-soie à mon avis. Venez la soie mes dents!

Let me help you with your bra: I am fully qualified.
Puis-je vous aider avec votre soutien-gorge: Je suis entièrement qualifié.

Getting around...
his and her body

You may think you're familiar with the human form from your collection of previous sexual encounters, but the French body presents a few unique attributes.

First of all there is the body hair. Don't be alarmed if you undress a French woman and it looks as if she still has a fur coat on. Hairy armpits are considered sexy in some European countries: the blacker the clump, the bigger the turn-on for those in-bred Mediterranean goat herders.

A French bloke may look as if the cigarette protruding from his mouth is part of his genetic make-up, but actually it's just a semi-permanent accessory (which may not be detached when he undresses). Other than that, the basic parts of the body should be vaguely recognisable to the trained eye.

Bodily parts:

Ankle
La cheville

Anus
L'anus (m)

Armpit
L'aisselle (f)

Arse
Le cul
La lune

Arsehole
Le trou de cul

Back
Le dos

Balls
Les testicules (m)
Les couilles
Les bijoux

Beard
La barbe
La barbouze

Belly
Le ventre
Le bide
Le bidon

Biceps
Les biceps (m)
Les biscoteaux (m)

Body
Le corps

Boobs
Les seins (m)
Les nichons (m)
Les miches (f)
Les tetons (m)
Les doudounes (f)

Brain
Le ciboulot
Les méninges

Bum
Le cul
Le derrière
Les fesses
Le derche
L'arrière-train

Buttocks
Les fesses (f)

Chest
La poitrine
Le coffre
La caisse

Chin
Le menton

Clit
Le clitoris

Sexy French

Cleavage
Le décolleté

Cock
La bite
La pine
La pipe
La queue
La verge
Le zob

Cunt
Le con

Dick
La quequette

Elbow
Le coude

Eye
Un œil

Getting around...his and her body

Eyes
Les yeux (m)
Les mirettes

Ears
Les oreilles (f)
Les esgourdes

Earlobes
Les lobes d'oreilles (m)

Face
La figure
Le visage
La gueule
La tronche
La bouille
La trogne

Fingers
Les doigts (m)

Foot
Le pied

Sexy French

Foreskin
Le prépuce

Genitalia
Les organes génitaux (m)
Le zizi

Guts
Les intestins (m)
Les boyeaux (m)
Les tripes (f)

Hair
Les cheveux (m)
Les tifs (m)

Hand
La main
La paluche
La pince
La patte

Head
La tête
La caboche
La fiole

Heart
Le coeur
Le palpitant

Heel
Le talon

Hips
Les hanches (f)

Knees
Les genoux (m)

Leg
La jambe
La patte
La guibole

Lips
Les lèvres (m)
Les babines (f)

Minge
La foufoune

Moustache
La moustache
Les bacchantes (f)

Mouth
La bouche
Le bec
La gueule

Navel
Le nombril

Neck
Le cou

Nipples
Les bouts de seins (m)

Nose
Le nez
Le pif

Getting around...his and her body

Nostrils
Les narines (f)

Paunch
La bedaine
La brioche

Pubes
Les poils du pubic (m)
La toison
La tarte aux poils

Pussy
La chatte
La foufoune

Skin
La peau

Shoulders
Les épaules

Teeth
Les dents (f)

Sexy French

Thighs
Les jambons
Les gigots

Thumb
La pouce

Toes
Les doigt de pieds (m)

Tongue
La langue

Waist
La taille
La ceinture

Wrists
Le poignet

Generic phrases:

Can I see your piercings?
Est-ce que je peux voir vos piercings?

You have a great body.
Vous avez un beau corps.

Ever thought about joining a gym?
Est-ce que vous avez considéré à joindre une salle de gym?

Have you ever considered using deodorant?
Avez-vous jamais considéré utiliser un déodorant?

Do you have any interesting tattoos?
Avez-vous des tattoos intéressants?

Sexy French

To him:

Lose the beard. It gives me thigh-rash.
Raser-vous la barbe. Elle me donne une éruption.

Does my bum look big in this?
Regardez mon cul: est-ce qu'il est trop grand.

Oh, there it is! I thought you were a girl at first.
Ah, c'est la! J'ai pensé d'abord que vous êtiez une
fille.

Oh, man-boobs. I thought they were a myth.
Ah, des seins de l'homme. J'ai pensé qu'ils etaient
un mythe.

**I will only suck your toes if you get that athlete's
foot treated.**
Je sucerai vos orteils si vous vous traitez le pied
d'athlète.

To her:

Your breasts are perfect.
Vos seins sont parfaits.

Can I nestle in your cleavage?
Est-ce que je peux me nicher dans votre fendage?

I really like your furry armpits.
J'aime vraiment vos aisselles plein de poils.

How on earth did you train your nipples to do that?
Comment diable avez-vous formé vos mamelons
pour faire cela?

Is it normal for women to have hair there?
Est-il normal que les femmes aient des poils là?

Getting laid...
how to get your leg over au Français

A sexual encounter with a French man is like unwrapping a particularly expensive and delicate soft cheese. Quite literally. But the smell goes once he's showered. Prepare for a vigorous and noisy session with someone who's convinced he's the greatest lover in the world: after all, he practises on his own every day.

Sex with a French woman is a more sensual, slow moving and graceful phenomenon, but it's still best to chuck her in the shower before you start, just to be on the safe side.

Key verbs:

To bugger
Emmancher
Enculer
Enfoirer

To come
Jouir
Prendre son pied

To copulate
Copuler

To do it doggy-style
Baiser en levrette

To deflower
Depuceler

To feel up
Faire des papouilles à

To fondle
Faire des mamours à

Getting laid...how to get your leg over au Français

To fornicate
Forniquer

To fuck
Baiser

To give a blow-job
Tailler une pipe

To kiss
Embrasser

To make love
S'envoyer
Se farcir
Se payer
Se taper

To pet
Se péloter

To play footsie with
Faire du pied à
Faire du genou à

Sexy French

To pounce on
Sauter sur

To seduce
Séduire

To snog
Se bécoter

Key nouns:

Bedroom
Le baisodrome

Buggery
La sodomie

Climax
L'extase
Un orgasme

Condoms
Des préservatifs
Des capotes anglaises

Cockteaser
Une allumeuse

Erotica films
Les films érotiques (m)

Erogenous zones
Les zones érogènes (f)

Sexy French

Kiss
Un bisou

Lovebite
Un suçon

Lovemaking
Les rapports sexuels (m)

Lubrication
Le graissage

Missionary position
La position du missionnaire

One-night stand
Une histoire d'une nuit

Post-coital fag
Une cigarette après l'amour

Rendezvous
Un rencard

Seductress
Une séductrice

Sex aid
Le gadget érotique

Sexual exploits
Les exploits (m)

Sexuality
La sexualité

Sexual orientation
L'orientation sexuelle (f)

69
Le soixante-neuf

Stiffy
Bander

Striptease
Un striptease
L'effeuilleuse (f)

Generic phrases:

Is it really necessary to be filming this?
Est-il vraiment nécessaire de filmer ceci?

Could you ask you mother to leave before I undress?
Pourriez-vous vous demander à votre mère de partir avant que je me déshabille?

A little bit more foreplay would be nice.
Un peu plus de préliminaires amoureux serait agréable.

Just move a little to the left: I can't see the TV.
Déplace-toi vers la gauche: je ne peux pas voir la télé.

To him:

Mmm, British men normally take a little more time.
Mmm, les hommes britanniques prennent
normalement un peu plus de temps.

I can still smell your Camembert.
Je peux encore sentir votre Camembert.

Is it in yet?
Est-il dedans encore?

To her:

Honestly, this is quite big where I come from.
Vraiment, c'est assez grand d'où je viens.

I am a self-taught gynaecologist.
Je suis un gynécologue autodidacte.

Getting up...
the morning after

Your head hurts. Other parts of your body ache. The sheets are soggy. You've woken up in a strange room with a strange French bed-partner. *Merde!* It seemed like a good idea at the time but now that you're sober, well - that's a different matter.

Generic phrases:

That was the best night of my life.
C'était la meilleure nuit de ma vie.

I'm sorry, I didn't realise you were French.
Je suis désolé, je n'avais pas réalisé que vous êtiez
Français.

Are you still here?
Êtes-vous toujours-là?

Can I see you again?
Est-ce que l'on peut se revoir?

Do you mind if we don't see each other again?
Est-ce que cela vous dérange si nous ne nous
revoyons pas?

To him:

Please put your pants on before my husband returns.
Habillez-vous avant que mon mari revienne.

Sorry about the sheets. I'm not due until next week.
Je suis désolée au sujet des draps de lit. D'habitude, mes règles viennent plus tard.

Oh, it was your bottom. I thought there had been a minor earthquake.
Ah, c'était votre cul. J'ai pensé qu'il y avait eu un petit tremblement de terre.

Thanks - you've helped convince me that I should become a lesbian.
Merci - vous m'avez convaincue que je devrais devenir une lesbienne.

Last night was an education: in my country it's customary to try the vagina first.
La nuit dernière était une nouvelle expérience: dans mon pays on utilise le vagin en premier.

To her:

Can you shave your legs next time?
Pouvez-vous raser vos jambes la prochaine fois?

That was so good, I feel I ought to pay you.
C'était si bon que je voudrais vous payer.

Looking at your face in the daylight I feel like I've committed bestiality.
Regardant votre visage au jour, c'est comme si j'avais commis la bestialité.

If you enjoyed that, remember to tell your friends.
Si vous aimez cela, n'oubliez pas de le dire à vos amis.

Although I told you I loved you, you will be receiving a letter from my solicitor retracting that statement.
Bien que je vous aie dit que je vous ai aimé, vous recevrez une lettre de mon avocat rétractant cette déclaration.

Getting desperate

Of course, even the smoothest chat-up lines
in this book won't work for everyone.
Perhaps you smell like a wilting slice of Brie?
Perhaps you're wearing union jack pants and a
t-shirt that says 'I hate France'? If so, you need
professional help. Paris and most other French
cities have thousands of prostitutes ready and
willing to give you that professional help. Go
for it!

At the brothel

Key words:

Brothel
La maison close
Le bordel

Pervert
Un pervers
Un obsédé sexuel

Prostitute
Une prostituée
Une pute

Sexual services
Le commerce sexuel

Sordid
Sordide

Whore
Une putain

Generic phrases:

Where is the local brothel?
Où est la maison close la plus proche?

I'm looking for some hot-prozzie action.
Je suis à la recherche de bons moments.

I've brought my own johnnies.
J'ai des preservatifs.

Do you do tricks?
Faites-vous des tours?

Is that legal?
C'est legal?

Would you mind taking a bath first?
Est-ce que cela vous dérangerait de prendre un bain d'abord?

A hand-job will do nicely, thanks.
Une branlette serait appréciable, merci.

How much for straight sex?
Combien pour la passe?

Getting desperate

Gimme a blow job.
Taillez-moi une pipe.

You should do more pelvic exercises: you're a bit slack downstairs.
Vous devriez faire plus d'exercices pelviens: vous êtes relâchée du bas.

When were these sheets last washed?
Quand est-ce que ces draps ont été lavés?

How much without the glove?
Combien sans la capote?

Oh, this is the first time I've seen a Brazilian wax.
Ah, c'est le premier fois que j'ai vu une foufoune rasée.

What percentage does your pimp take?
Quel pourcentage votre macro prend-il?

Is the Marquis de Sade a chum of yours?
Marquis de Sade est-il un ami à vous?

Are you on The Pill?
Prennez-vous la pilule?

How many partners have you had?
Combien d'amants avez-vous eus?

Sexy French

Do you swing both ways?
Etes-vous les deux?

Are there any lesbians available for the night?
Y a-t-il des lesbiennes disponibles pour la nuit?

How many abortions have you had?
Combien d'avortements avez-vous eu?

Where are the keys to these handcuffs?
Où sont les clés de ces menottes?

Keep that vibrator away from me. It looks lethal.
Eloignez ce vibrateur de moi. Il est mortel.

I've never done this before.
Je n'ai jamais fait ceci avant.

Can we just talk?
Pouvons-nous juste parler?

Do you take Traveller's Cheques?
Acceptez-vous les chèques-voyage?

The murky world of porn

Can I get a student discount?
Est-ce que je peux obtenir une remise d'étudiant?

Will this show up on my credit card statement?
Est-ce que ceci apparaîtra sur mon relevé de carte de crédit?

Are you showing anything with 70s tits, like Emmanuelle?
Montrez-vous quelque chose avec des seins des années soixante-dix, comme Emmanuelle?

Are all the seats as sticky as this one?
Sont-ils tous les sièges aussi collants que celui-ci?

Do you have any private wanking booths?
Avez-vous des cabines de branlantes privées?

When does the next peep show start?
Quand le prochain piaulement montre-t-il le début?

Which screen is showing the animal film?
Sur quel écran est le film d'animaux?

Can I have a refund please? I didn't realise that this film was for benders.
Est-ce que je peux avoir un remboursement s'il vous plaît? Je pas me rendais par compte que ce film était pour des cintreuses.

Do you mind if I have a wank?
Est-ce que cela vous dérange si j'ai une branlette?

Where can I buy some man-size tissues?
Où puis-je acheter des tissus plus grand?

Getting it cured

It's common knowledge that France is about as disease-free as an Iraqi biological weapons factory. If you found the previous chapter helpful, you'll almost certainly need a visit to the doctor around about now. Whatever form of pestilence you manage to contract, there are certain phrases that will prove invaluable when trying to dissuade a French doctor from shoving his stinky digits up your hole.

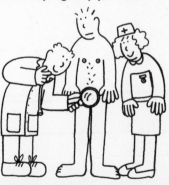

Abortion
Un avortement

Doctor
Un docteur

Nurse
Une infirmière

Doctor's surgery
Le cabinet médical

The hospital
L'hôpital (m)

Prescription
L'ordonnance (f)

AIDS
SIDA

The clap
La chtouille
La chaude-pisse
La vérole

Chlamydia
La chlamydia

Cystitis
La cystite

Genital warts
Les vésicules génitaux (f)

Gonorrheah
La blennorragie

Menstrual cramps
Les règles

Pregnant
Enceinte

Sexually transmitted disease
La maladie sexuellement transmissible

Smear test
Le frottis

Thrush
Les mycoses

Vaginal discharge
Les pertes blanches (f)

Venereal disease
La maladie vénérienne

Generic:

I'm rather itchy.
Ca me gratte.

I'm quite raw.
Je suis tout à fait cru.

It hurts when I piss.
Cela me fait mal quand je pisse.

What are these things in my pubes?
Quelles sont ces choses dans mes poils?

We have a history of syphilis in the family.
Nous avons une histoire du syphilis dans la famille.

For her:

I think I might be pregnant. No, I don't know who the father is.
Je pense que je pourrais être enceinte. Non, je ne sais pas qui est le père.

Can I have the morning after pill please?
Est-ce que je peux avoir la pilule du lendemain s'il vous plaît?

Is it really necessary to fondle me like that? I've only got a sore throat.
Est-il vraiment nécessaire de me toucher comme cela? J'ai seulement mal à la gorge.

My arse was a one-way street until last night. I think there's been a serious road accident.
Mon cul était une rue à sens unique jusqu'à la nuit passée. Je pense qu'il y a été un accident de la route sérieux.

Sexy French

Can you recommend any back-street abortionists?
Pouvez-vous recommander une faiseuse d'ange.

Are the knitting needles clean?
Les aiguilles à tricoter sont-elles propres?

The bleeding won't stop.
Le saignement ne s'arrêtera pas.

Apparently it's slightly fishy.
Apparemment ça sent le poisson.

No doctor, the other hole.
No docteur, l'autre trou, s'il vous plâit.

Must you use your tongue? My doctor in England uses a spatula.
Devez-vous utiliser votre langue? Mon docteur en Angleterre utilise une spatule.

For him:

I'd like some extra large condoms please.
Je voudrais des préservatifs extra larges, s'il vous plaît.

I think that whore has given me the clap.
Je pense que la putain m'a donné la chaude-pisse.

I didn't know she had a pierced clit. Please be careful when you remove the plaster.
Je ne savais pas qu'elle avait le clitoris percé.
Veuillez faire attention quand vous enlevez le pansement adhésif.

Of course we had safe sex, doctor. I locked the door myself.
Naturellement nous étions protégés, docteur.
J'avais verrouillé la porte moi-même.

It's a bit embarrassing really.
C'est un peu embarrassant vraiment.

Promise not to laugh?
Promettez-moi de ne pas rire?

Are you sure you need to see it?
Êtes-vous sûr vous devez le voir?

Someone spiked my drinks. Can you tell me if I lost my anal virginity last night?
Quelqu'un a empoisonné ma boisson. Pouvez-vous me dire si j'ai perdu ma virginité anale la nuit passée?

I wouldn't normally have done it, but the farmer wasn't looking. Can you remove the wool or will you refer me to a vet?
Je ne l'aurais pas normalement fait, mais le fermier ne regardait pas. Pouvez-vous enlever la laine ou préférez-vous me mettre en rapport avec un vétérinaire?

You're still holding onto my nuts.
Vous tenez toujours mes couilles en main.

Getting out...
of a relationship

With a nifty little book like this, the odds are
that your charms will prove irresistable to the
Frenchies, but let's face it - all you really
wanted was a one-night stand and now look
what a mess you're in. Just as well we have a
stock of trusty standard phrases that have
been helping fools like you extricate
themselves from unwanted love clinches for
centuries. In my early twenties, I dated a
charming young garçon on a camping holiday
in France. The courtship was shortlived,
naturally: I was clutching at straws - which is
far too apt an analogy. If only I'd known then
how to say 'Is that a tic-tac in your pocket or
are you just pleased to see me?'

Go on: shake that deluded, love-blind Frog
from your back forever. Bon chance!

Keywords:

Injunction
L'injonction (f)

Sexual harrassment
Le harcèlement sexuel

Phrases:

We need to talk.
Nous devons parler.

It's not you - it's me.
Ce n'est pas vous - c'est moi.

I'm married.
Je suis marié.

You're too good for me.
Vous êtes trop bien pour moi.

It's for the best.
C'est pour le meilleur.

It's just that you're French.
C'est juste que vous êtes français.

I need space.
J'ai besoin d'espace.

It's not working.
Ça ne marche pas.

I need my independence.
J'ai besoin de mon indépendance.

Let's be friends.
Soyons amis.

Let's meet again...in about forty years.
Revoyons-nous... dans environ quarante années.

I'm sorry, it's over.
Je suis désolé, c'est fini.

I'm seeing someone else.
Je vois quelqu'un d'autre.

I have a slightly more fragrant partner in England.
J'ai un(e) amant(e) un peu plus aromatisé en
Angleterre.

Please could you spell-check my suicide note?
S'il vous plaît pourriez-vous examiner ma note de
suicide?

**Is that a tic-tac in your pocket or are you just
pleased to see me?**
Est-ce que c'est un tic-tic-tac dans votre poche ou
êtes-vous juste heureux de me voir?

Getting away...
from a sticky situation

Making a quick getaway from an unpleasant
relationship disaster is one of the challenges
and joys of attempting to get it on in France.
Given that French marital fidelity is about as
rare as French vegetarianism, you're highly
likely to end up involved in a dangerous love
triangle. When the husband or wife returns
home unexpectedly, you need to act fast.
Learn these lifesaving phrases and try to avoid
getting caught with your pants round your
ankles (unless you're having a wee, in which
case you're forgiven but a little more
discretion wouldn't go amiss).

Some phrases that you hopefully won't have to use:

Damn! The fuzz are coming!
Sacrebleu! Les flics se portent!

He's a crazy stalker.
C'est un détraqué mental.

He's unconscious.
Il était dans le cirage.

I don't want a row, but if you don't shut up I'll give you another black eye.
Je ne veux pas une prise de bec, mais si vous ne fermez votre bouche, je vous donne un pain.

You deserve a kick in the arse.
Vous méritez que je vous files un coup de pied au cul.

Getting away...from a sticky situation

Stop squabbling!
Ne vous chamaillez pas!

I want to punch someone.
Je voudrais donner un coup de poing à quelqu'un.

I didn't know she was your daughter.
Je ne savais pas que c'était votre fille.

Are you trying to tell me she was a virgin?
Essayez-vous de me dire qu'elle était vierge?

I thought you French people were always unfaithful.
J'ai pensé que les français étaient toujours infidèles.

Where is the window?
Où est la fenêtre?

Please put the knife down.
Veuillez mettre le couteau vers le bas.

Sexy French

I'd rather not involve your poodle: it isn't hygienic.
Pas avec votre chien: il n'est pas hygiénique.

Where can I hide from your husband?
Où puis-je me cacher de votre mari?

Honey, I can explain . . .
Mon amour, je peux expliquer. . .

You bastard, I'll smash your face in.
Espece de salaud, je vais vous casser la gueule.

Put the gun down and walk away.
Mettez le pistolet vers le bas et vas-t'en.

What are French prisons like?
À quoi ressemblent les prisons françaises?

Get out!
Allez, oust!
Bouge de la!
Dégagez!
Debarrassez le plancher!

Getting away...from a sticky situation

I promise not to return to France if you don't hurt me.
Je promets de ne pas retourner en France si vous ne me blessez pas.

Please don't use the rubber gloves, officer. I was joking about the cocaine.
Veuillez ne pas utiliser les gants en caoutchouc, officier. Je plaisantais au sujet de la cocaïne.

I hate you!
Je vous déteste!

You bastard!
Salopard!

Fuck off!
Foutre le camp!
Va te faire foutre!

What a shitty thing to say.
C'est dégueulasse de dire ça.

Shit!
Merde!

Getting hitched

The worst case scenario...all of your escape
attempts have failed and you feel you must
marry a French type. How should one go
about popping *le question*? Or perhaps, worse
still, a French person decides to propose to
you. What can one say to such an affront to
your personal liberty?

Generic:

There's something I need to ask you.
Il y a quelque chose que je dois vous demander.

Will you marry me?
Veux-tu m'épouser?

I want to meet your parents.
Je veux rencontrer vos parents.

I want to spend the rest of my life with you, despite the fact you're French.
Je veux passer le reste de ma vie avec vous, en dépit du fait que vous êtes français.

We've sold the rights to Okay! magazine.
Nous avons vendu les droits à Okay! magazine.

Get me to the church on time.
Ammenez-moi à l'église à l'heure.

I'll marry you as long as we can keep it a secret from my mates.
Je vous épouserai si nous pouvons le garder le secret.

I've spoken to my accountant and he says I should marry you for tax purposes.
J'ai parlé à mon comptable et il dit que je dois vous épouser pour des impôts.

It's a shot-gun wedding.
C'est un marriage forcé.

I don't believe in sex before marriage. Let's get married...now!
Je ne crois pas au sexe avant mariage. Marions-nous...maintenant!

For her:

Why are you on your knees?
Pourquoi êtes-vous sur vos genoux?

The answer is no - unless you come up with a bigger diamond.
La réponse est non - à moins que vous fournissez un plus grand diamant.

You must be joking!
Vous devez plaisanter!

But you're my brother!
Mais vous êtes mon frère!

I'm not sure, let me check my diary first.
Je ne suis pas sûr, je dois regarder mon agenda d'abord.

Sexy French

For him:

Can I have your daughter's hand in marriage?
Est-ce que je peux avoir la main de votre fille en
mariage?

How can you justify a white wedding?
Comment pouvez-vous justifier un mariage en
blanc?

What do you mean, you're pregnant?
Que voulez-vous dire, vous êtes en enceinte?

But I thought you were on The Pill.
Mais je pensais que vouz prenniez la pilule.

How much is that diamond ring?
Combien coûte cette bague en diamant?

Some other useful words:

Divorce
Le divorce

Lawyer
Un avocat

Presents
Les cadeaux (m)

Trial separation
La séparation

Wedding ring
Une alliance

Wedding vows
Les vœux de mariage (m)

Getting home

At the end of your adventures in France, you'll be longing for the comforts of proper chips, safer roads, real beer and brown sauce. You'll also be ready to appreciate once more the benefits of a relationship with someone with whom you can actually communicate. You'll look forward to enjoying the sight of women who don't spend half their time at the hairdressers getting their armpits trimmed, or to revelling in the presence of normal, spotty men who know they're crap in bed and don't bother to pretend otherwise. It's therefore vital to get out of France as quickly as possible and back to civilisation.

Keywords:

Where is the station?
Où est la gare?

Where is the airport?
Où est l'aéroport?

Where is the ferry terminal?
Où est le bac?

Here is my passport.
Voici mon passeport.

I have nothing to declare...except the disease I caught from one of your prostitutes.
Je n'ai rien à déclarer... sauf la maladie que j'ai attrapé avec une prostituée française.

Where can I change these Euros into proper money?
Où puis-je changer ces Euros en réel argent?

Sexy French

My lover has left me. Can I change my ticket to an earlier flight home?
Mon fiancé m'a quitté. Est-ce que je peux changer mon billet pour un vol plus tôt?

1000 cigarettes and a bottle of gin, please.
Mille cigarettes et une bouteille de gin, s'il vous plaît.

How many porn videos can I bring back?
Combien de films pornographiques est-ce que je peux rapporter?

Please stop kicking the back of my seat.
Cessez de donner un coup de pied le dos de mon siège, s'il vous plaît.

Please don't talk to me in French: I have a black belt in xenophobia.
S'il vous plaît ne me parlez pas en français: j'ai une ceinture noire en xénophobie.

Well done! You serve proper chips on this ferry.
Bien fait! Vous servez des vrais frites sur ce ferry.

Getting home

Get me out of this shit-hole of a country.
Sauvez-moi de ce pays de merde.

I'll bloody well stick to Scarborough next year.
J'irai à Scarborough l'année prochaine.

Would you like to join the Mile High Club with me, even though we're on a boat?
Voulez-vous rejoindre le club de haut de mille avec moi, quoique nous soyons sur un bâteau?

Bonnes vacances!

The Little Book of Essential Foreign Swearwords

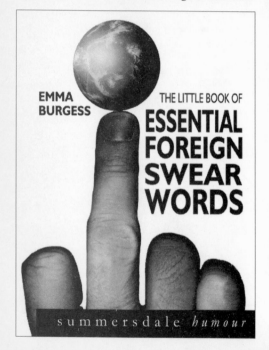

EMMA
BURGESS

THE LITTLE BOOK OF

**ESSENTIAL
FOREIGN
SWEAR
WORDS**

summersdale humour

The Little Book of Flirting

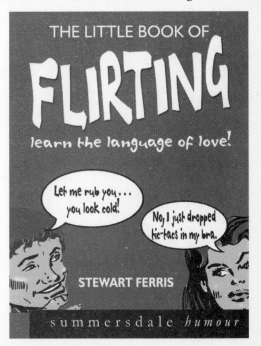

**For the latest humour books
from Summersdale, check out**

www.summersdale.com